theory for piano students

by LORA BENNER

BOOK
THREE

ED. 2525

G. SCHIRMER, *Inc.*

DISTRIBUTED BY

HAL•LEONARD®
CORPORATION
7777 W. BLUEMOUND RD. P.O. BOX 13819 MILWAUKEE, WI 53213

FOREWORD

This book provides theoretic knowledge, writing, and playing experience in musical subjects which are related to the third year of piano study.

The scope of the material may be increased by:

1. Writing additional intervals and chords.

2. Identifying intervals and chords by sound.

3. Analyzing other easy folk songs and good classics:
   a) Writing numerals under the harmony.
   b) Identifying the main cadences.
   c) Identifying temporary modulation.
   d) Counting according to the meter and melodic rhythm.

4. Examining compositions for simple and compound meter and regular and irregular accents.

5. Playing compositions of various composers and discussing their individual characteristics.

L. B.

CONTENTS

Lesson One

RELATIVE MINOR SCALES

We have learned that there are 15 Key Signatures for 15 Major Keys. These same Key Signatures also stand for 15 Minor Scales or Keys.

A Major and a Minor which have the **SAME KEY SIGNATURE** are called **RELATIVES**. They are related by Key Signature.

To find the relative minor of a major, count down to *la*. This is *do* of the minor.

Large letters are used for Majors.
Small letters are used for minors.

Here is the circle of fifths for the Relative Majors and Minors.

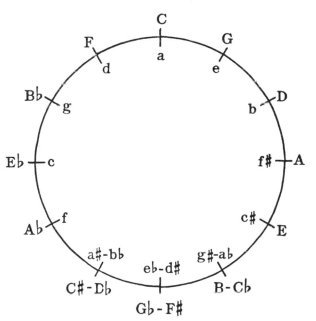

Write the Major and Minor Key-tones for each Key Signature.

The NATURAL MINOR SCALE is the same as the Major Scale (no accidentals) except that it is from *la* to *la* of the major. The ascending (going up) scale is seldom used because of the whole step between 7 and 8.

The TWO most frequently used minor scales are:

1. The HARMONIC MINOR which raises the 7th Scale degree one half-step by an accidental sharp or natural sign to make a half-step between 7 - 8. This is the minor scale usually found in piano music.

2. The MELODIC MINOR which raises both the 6th and 7th Scale degrees one half-step by accidental sharps or natural signs.... GOING UP ONLY. Going down, the Natural Minor scale is used. The interval between 6 and 7 of the Harmonic Minor of one and one half-steps is difficult to sing. The Melodic Minor is used for vocal music and some other instrumental music. It is occasionally found in piano music.

These examples are the scales of *A minor* – relative of *C major*. Play all three forms using the same fingering as *A major*.

On the staffs below: Write the key signatures in sharps.
Write the HARMONIC minor scales
one octave up and down.
Put in the accidentals both up and down.
In the scales of g♯ and d♯ use × for
the accidental.

3

a

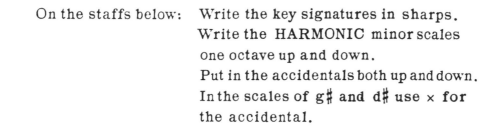

e: 1♯

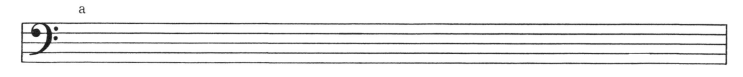

b: 2♯s

f♯ : 3♯s

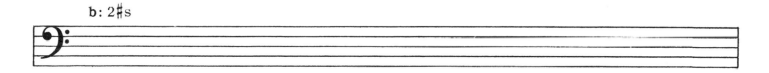

c♯ : 4♯s

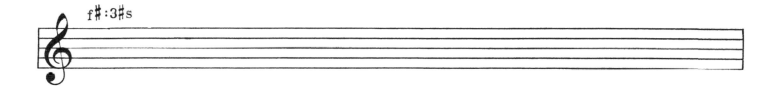

g♯ : 5♯s

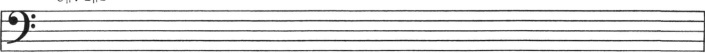

d♯ : 6♯s

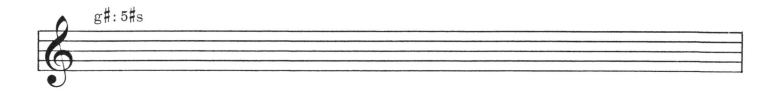

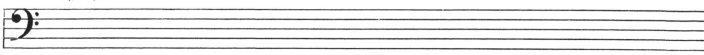

4

On the staffs below: Write the key signatures in flats.
Write the HARMONIC minor scales
one octave up and down.
Put in the accidentals both up and down.
Be sure to check the key signatures to
see whether to use a sharp or a natural
sign to raise 7.

d: 1♭

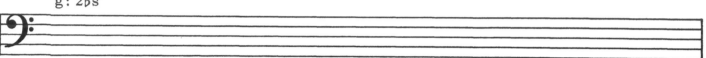

g: 2♭s

c: 3♭s

f: 4♭s

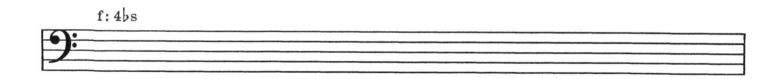

b♭: 5♭s

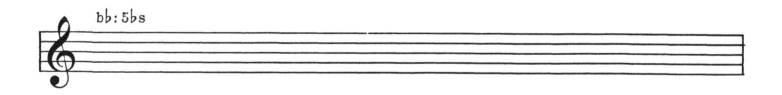

e♭: 6♭s

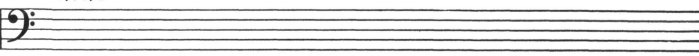

On the staffs below write the MELODIC minor scales one octave up and down for the key signatures indicated. Write in the key signatures.

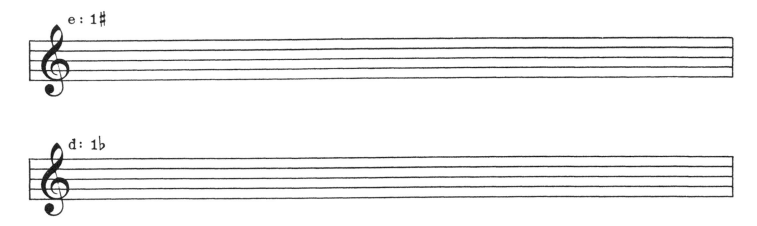

To find the RELATIVE MAJOR of a given minor scale, count up to *mi* for *do* of the Major Scale.

Write the relative MAJOR *do* for each minor *do* given. Use capital letters for the Majors.

a = _____   f = _____   b = _____   d = _____   c = _____

b♭ = _____   f♯ = _____   c♯ = _____   e = _____   g = _____

e♭ = _____   a♯ = _____   a♭ = _____

Fill in the Key-tones for the Relative Major and Minor Scales on the Circle of Fifths.

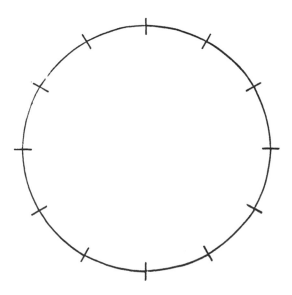

Work Sheet

1   What do a Major and its RELATIVE Minor Scale have in common?

_____

2   What THREE kinds of minor scales are mentioned in this lesson?_____

_____

3   If you know the name of the Major Scale how do you find *do* of the relative Minor Scale?

_____

4   Which Scale Degree is raised in the Harmonic Minor Scale?

_____

5   Which Scale Degrees are raised in the ASCENDING Melodic Minor Scale?

_____

6   Which minor scale is used for the DESCENDING Melodic Minor Scale?

_____

7   Why is the Harmonic Minor Scale not used in vocal music?

_____

8   Write the relative Key-tones for those given.

a)   F_____   G_____   D_____   E_____

b)   f_____   g_____   d_____   e_____

9   Write the Key-tones in the spaces below:

M   m   M   m   M   m   M   m

Lesson Two

PARALLEL MINORS

PARALLEL MINORS and MAJORS have the SAME Key-tone, *do* - C major and
C minor are parallel.

These are also called by other names: Corresponding, Homotonic, etc., but their
relationship is the same.

Parallel majors and minors do NOT have the same key signature. Parallel minors
have THREE Flats more or three sharps less (or two of one and one of the
other) in their key signatures.

Below are the parallel minors with some of the key signatures given. Write in the others.

Minor scales are usually fingered the same as their Parallel Majors.

Minor keys are often used for sad or mysterious music.

Play the major and minor triads written below. Listen to them so that your ear can tell
whether a triad is major or minor. Notice that the 3rd is lowered by a ♭ or ♮ in the minor triad.

On the staff below, write the key signatures for the MINOR Key-tones given.

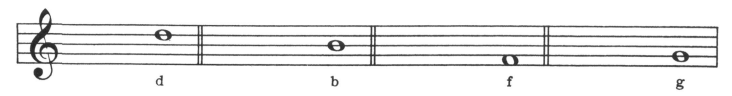

d   b   f   g

On the following staff, write the MINOR Key-tones for the Key Signatures given.

Below are Major Triads. Write the Minor Triad for each in the space after each chord. Lower the third one half-step.

Write the Minor Triads, first inversion, for the Major Triads given below. Notice that the third to be lowered one half-step is at the bottom of the chord.

Play all of the triads given above. Then play their second inversions without music.

Minor Intervals

In Book 2 we learned that Intervals of a Major Scale on the tonic *(do)* are either PERFECT or MAJOR.

PERFECT INTERVALS are 1 4 5 8

MAJOR INTERVALS are 2 3 6 7

Mark the intervals below M or P and the size of each.

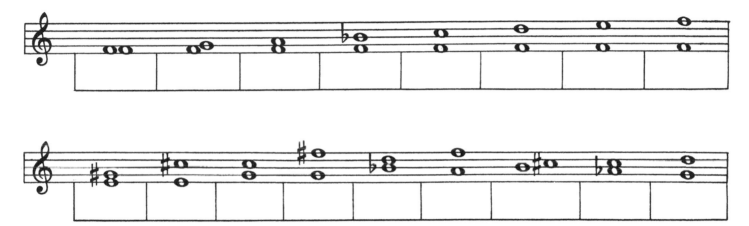

MAJOR INTERVALS which are made one half-step smaller without changing the letter names are MINOR INTERVALS.

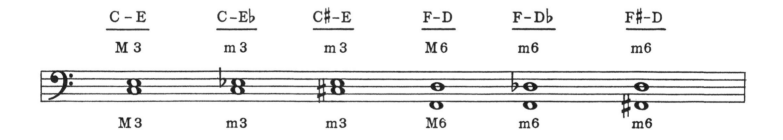

Mark the intervals below M or m and their size.

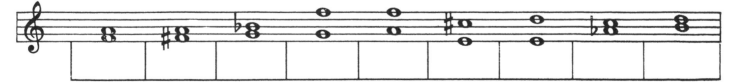

Work Sheet

1   What is the same for PARALLEL Major and Minor Scales?

_____

2   What is the difference in their Key Signatures?

_____

3   On the staff below are Major Key Signatures.

Write in the Parallel Minor Signatures for each.

4   On the staff below are Key-tones. Write the Major and Parallel Minor Key Signatures

for each.

5   On the staff below, write minor intervals two ways for each major interval given.

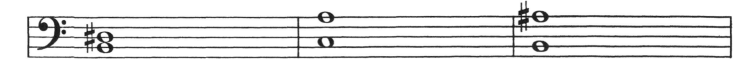

6   How much smaller is a minor interval than a major interval?

_____

Work Sheet

7   On the staff below, write major and minor triads in ROOT POSITION on the notes given. Add 2 notes.

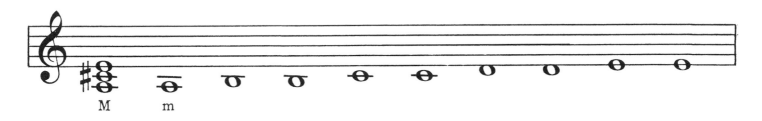

8   On the following staff, write the major and minor triads in the FIRST INVERSION on the notes given.

9   On the following staff, write the major and minor triads in the SECOND INVERSION on the notes given.

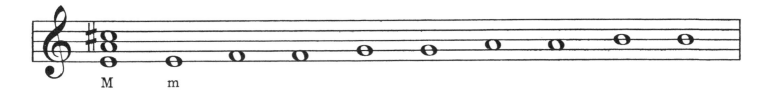

10 What note of a triad is lowered one half-step to make it minor?

_____

Lesson Three

FRANZ PETER SCHUBERT

(1797 - 1828)

Six years after Mozart died in Vienna, Schubert was born there. His father was a schoolmaster. By the time Franz was ten years old, he played the violin, piano and organ. He also had a fine singing voice.

When he was eleven years old, he was a free board pupil in a school for boy singers. His first music teacher there said, "the boy knows everything already."

His voice changed when he was sixteen; and although he was a musical genius, his other studies were not good enough to enable him to get a scholarship to continue in school.

When he was nineteen years old, he went to live with a friend who realized that Franz was one of the greatest and most talented musicians who ever lived. He was a very simple and childlike person. He has been called the "least schooled of the great musicians."

He lived a rather routine life. He would get up in the morning and compose for six or seven hours and write very rapidly without rechecking his work. If during an evening someone suggested to him that it would be good if he wrote a symphony, he would write one the next day!

His friends loved to sing his beautiful songs. Poets were honored to provide lyrics for them. He was the greatest song writer who ever lived.

He wrote a great deal of music during his short life — over 634 songs for solo voice and piano in addition to piano compositions, string quartets, symphonies, operas, masses, chamber music, and many other compositions.

When Beethoven died, Schubert was in the funeral procession. A year later he died and was buried near Beethoven.

Ten years after his death, Schumann heard that there were many Schubert manuscripts lying around Vienna. He found many of them, including the great *C Major Symphony*. Felix Mendelssohn conducted the first performance of this symphony.

Brahms helped edit an edition of Schubert's work which contains over forty volumes!

Major and Minor Triads

We have worked with the I, IV and V chords in Major Keys. We have also written and
played these triads in Root Position, First Inversion (the 6 chord) and Second
Inversion (the $\frac{6}{4}$ chord).

On the staff below write triads in three positions for C, F and G.

Then play them on the piano.

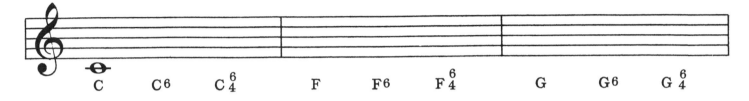

On the following staff write triads in three positions for the Tonic, Subdominant and Dominant notes of the Major Key given. Play them on the piano.

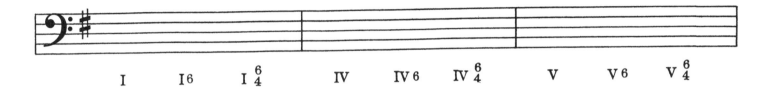

Now write them for the Key of F Major and play them.

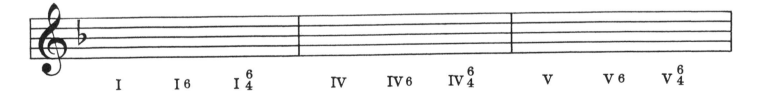

We can easily see and hear that these are all MAJOR TRIADS. A Major triad has a
major 3rd and a perfect 5th above the root.

The I, IV and V triads of any Major Key are Major triads.

Play them in other Major Keys.

A MINOR TRIAD has a minor 3rd and a perfect 5th above the root.

In Minor Keys, the triads on I and IV are minor. The triad on V is major because of the
7th which is raised by the accidental.

Using A Minor as our example, we find:
The tonic triad of 1 3 5 is minor.
The subdominant triad of 4 6 8 is minor.
The dominant triad of 5 7 2 is major.

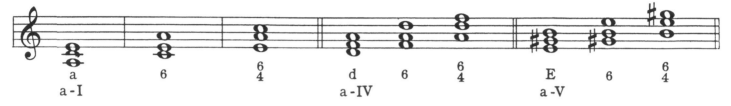

On the staff below, write these three principal triads in three positions in the key of
E Minor

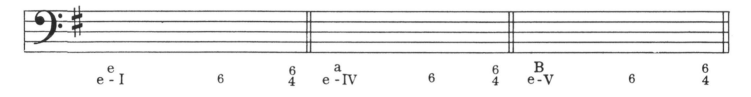

On the staff below, write these three principal triads and their inversions in the key of
D Minor.

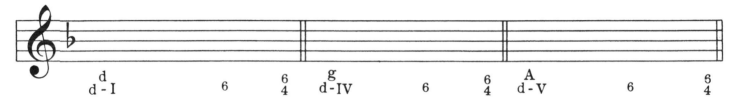

Play these triads. Then play them in other minor keys.

Below is a part of *The Wild Horseman* by Robert Schumann.

In what key is this part written?

Write in the time signature and mark I, IV or V under the chords.

Study the Scale of Triads for the C Major Scale given below. Notice that the triads on D, E and A are minor because they have the interval of a *minor* third from the bottom note to the middle note. However, there is a PERFECT fifth from the bottom note to the top note (except VII).

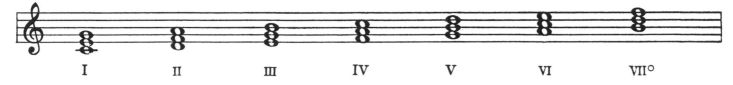

I   II   III   IV   V   VI   VII°

The triads of a major key on the following scale degrees are minor:

    Supertonic II

    Mediant III

    Submediant VI

The minor triads are marked by small Roman Numerals.

Notice the triad on B for the Scale of Triads above. This triad has a minor third from the bottom to the middle note and a diminished fifth from the bottom to the top note. It is called a diminished triad.

When a PERFECT INTERVAL is made one half-step smaller but keeps the same letter names, it becomes a DIMINISHED INTERVAL. The symbol for the diminished interval is °.

Write the Scale of Triads for the Key of G Major. Under each triad write the large or small Roman numeral and the diminished sign for the triad on the 7th scale degree. Play these triads.

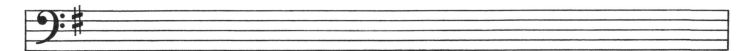

Do the same for the Key of F Major.

Play the scale of triads in other Major Keys.

Now we shall see that using minor chords where we can, improves the harmony for *America*.

Play this on the piano.

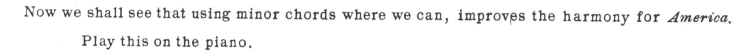

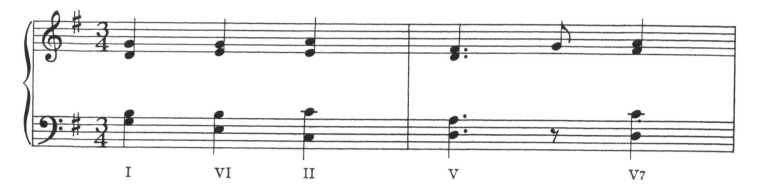

I   VI   II   V   V7

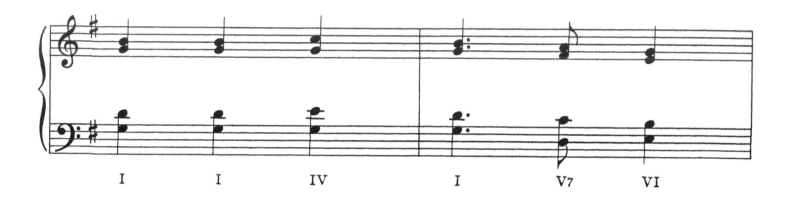

I   I   IV   I   V7   VI

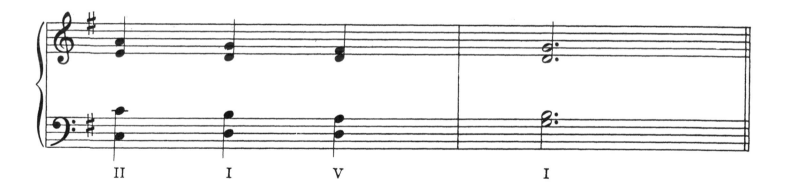

II   I   V   I

What is the Cadence formed by the last two chords?

_____

Check if it is Perfect _____ or Imperfect _____

On the staves below, write in the time signature and mark the numerals and inversions under the chords. Play this music on the piano. Do you know the name of this song? Can you transpose it to other keys?

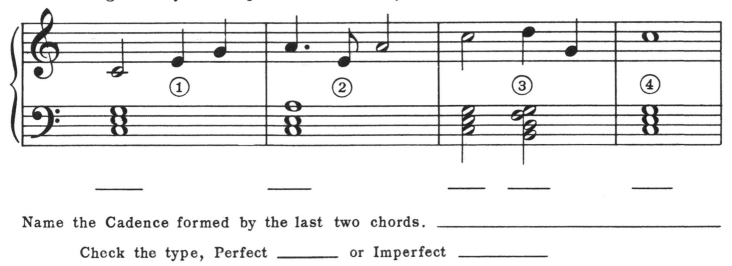

Name the Cadence formed by the last two chords. _____

Check the type, Perfect _____ or Imperfect _____

On the staves below, (1) write the key signature, (2) the time signature, (3) mark the numerals and inversions under the chords (where not given), (4) play this music. Do you know the name of it? Can you transpose it to other keys?

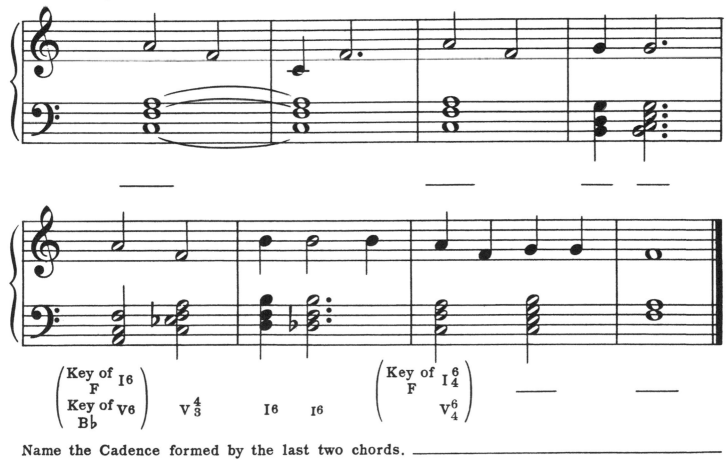

Name the Cadence formed by the last two chords. _____

Check the type, Perfect _____ or Imperfect _____

Work Sheet

1 On the staff below, write the Scale of Triads for D Major. Use accidentals. Mark the
   Triads with Roman Numerals. Use large numerals for Majors, small numerals for
   minors, and the diminished sign °

2 On the staff below, write the Scale of Triads for Bb Major and use accidentals. Mark
   the numerals under each triad.

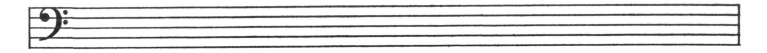

3 Who was called the "least schooled of the great musicians?" Give his first and last names
   and the town where he was born.

   _____

4 Which Scale Degrees of Major Scales are the ROOTS of MAJOR TRIADS?

   _____

5 Which Scale Degrees of Major Scales are the ROOTS of MINOR TRIADS?

   _____

6 Why is the Triad on VII a diminished triad?

   _____

7 How is the diminished figure written? _____

Lesson Four

FELIX MENDELSSOHN

(1809-1847)

Felix Mendelssohn was born in Hamburg, Germany. His parents were wealthy people who loved music and art. His mother taught him and his elder sister, Fanny, to play the piano.

When he was only nine years old, Felix gave a concert. He also began composing music while very young. His parents helped him in every possible way to develop his talents. Sundays at their home, a small orchestra met and performed music. Since the orchestra often played the compositions Felix had written, it was a great help to him to hear them soon after they were written.

By the time he was seventeen, his compositions were masterful. At this age he wrote the *Overture to a Midsummer Night's Dream,* which is one of the very greatest overtures in all music. One of the pieces from this music is the famous Wedding March.

Felix was also talented in art and in writing. He had a fine education which included study at the University of Berlin. He gave concerts all over Europe, conducting orchestras and playing the piano. Everyone loved him because he was such a fine person and good musician.

Mendelssohn helped many other musicians become known in England and other European countries by introducing and playing their compositions. He was the first to play Beethoven's *Emperor Concerto* in England. He made people know of Bach's greatness when he conducted the *St. Matthew Passion.*

He also formed the famous conservatory at Leipzig by organizing a fine orchestra there and bringing in other famous musicians to teach at the school.

Mendelssohn loved his family. He was happily married and the father of five children. However, he was not strong. He died at the age of thirty-eight.

Cadences - Chord Progressions

TRIADS are the basis of our harmonic system. Most of our musical compositions are written on chords.

CHORD PROGRESSION is the way chords move from one chord to another. Being able to recognize the important chord progressions is a great help in learning music.

In Book 2 we began the study of cadences. CADENCES are musical punctuation. They are important chord progressions of two or more chords. The final chord is called the CADENCE CHORD.

AUTHENTIC CADENCES are chord progressions of V to I. On the staff below, write the authentic cadences marked.

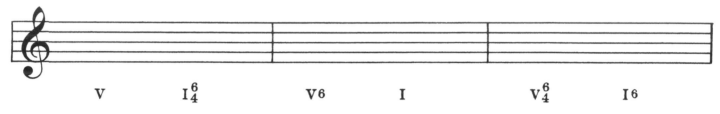

$$\text{V} \qquad \text{I}_4^6 \qquad \text{V6} \qquad \text{I} \qquad \text{V}_4^6 \qquad \text{I6}$$

Play these chords first with the right hand alone. Then play with both hands having the left hand play the ROOTS (V or I) of the chords.

Write the following cadences. Then play them in the same manner.

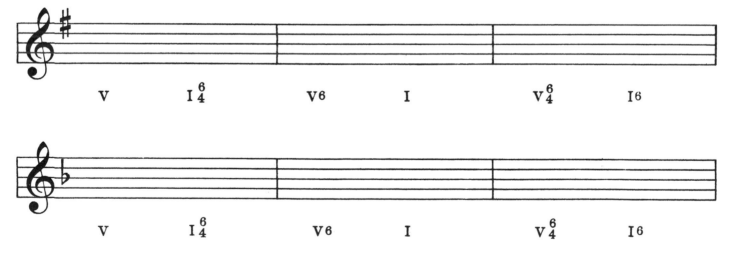

$$\text{V} \qquad \text{I}_4^6 \qquad \text{V6} \qquad \text{I} \qquad \text{V}_4^6 \qquad \text{I6}$$

$$\text{V} \qquad \text{I}_4^6 \qquad \text{V6} \qquad \text{I} \qquad \text{V}_4^6 \qquad \text{I6}$$

Can you play authentic cadences in all Major Keys this way?

PERFECT CADENCES have the KEY TONE (do) in the soprano and bass of the Cadence chord. Which inversions of the V and I chords make a perfect cadence? _____

Authentic Cadences in Minor Keys have the same Roots and the same V or V7 chords as their Parallel Majors. The Cadence Chord is the minor tonic triad. Examine, then play the C Major and C Minor Authentic Cadences below.

C Major

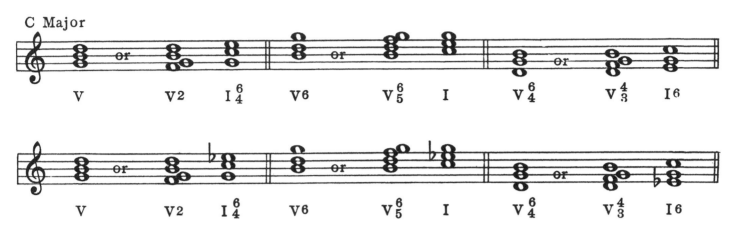

Play the Parallel Major and Minor Authentic Cadences in all keys. Use both hands. Play the V I roots with the Left Hand.

Plagal Cadences

Plagal Cadences are chord progressions from IV to I. This cadence is used at the close of hymns for the AMEN. It is usually in Major when so used.

On the staff below, mark the numerals and inversions for the Plagal Cadences given. Play the chords with the Right Hand and add the roots (IV I) with the Left Hand. Then play them in the minor key by using the accidentals in ( )s.

Write the following Plagal Cadences in Major Keys. Then play them in Major and Parallel Minor keys with both hands: Right Hand for chords, Left Hand for roots.

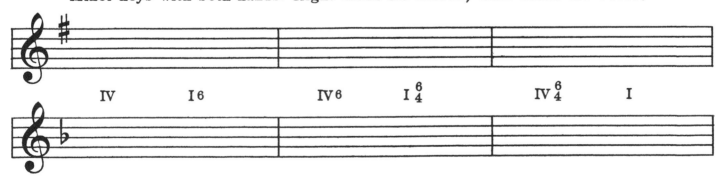

In the same way play the Plagal cadences in all Major and Minor Keys.

Authentic and Plagal Cadences are often combined with the Plagal Cadence first, then the
Authentic Cadence: IV I   V   I. This is called an **EXTENDED AUTHENTIC
CADENCE.**

The following is part of the *Sonatina in G* by Beethoven. Play this on the piano. Notice the
chord progressions. Notice that the last two measures form an extended authentic
cadence. Notice also that while the melody has notes from these chords, there are
also other notes which are not in the chords but which link them together. These other
tones are called *non-chordic tones* because they are not part of the chord.

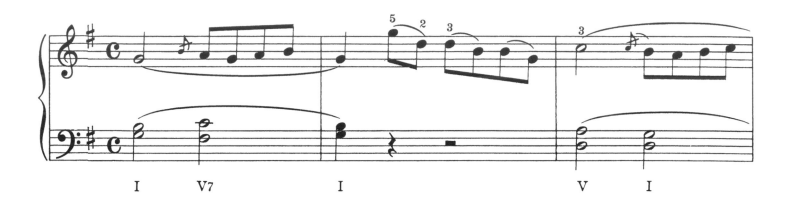

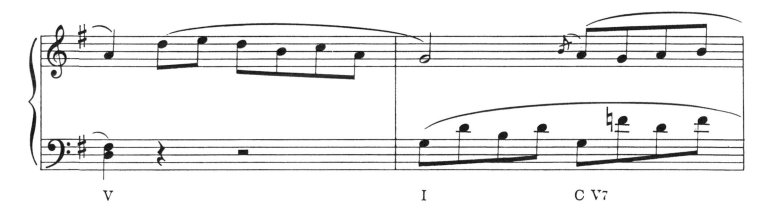

Any cadence which has more than two chords is a MIXED CADENCE. Below is *America the Beautiful*. Write in the bass chords above the numerals. Where there are two numeral and inversion figures in ( )s, they refer to only one chord. The chords of the last two measures form a frequently found mixed cadence.

$$I \qquad V_4^6 \qquad V_5^6 \qquad I$$

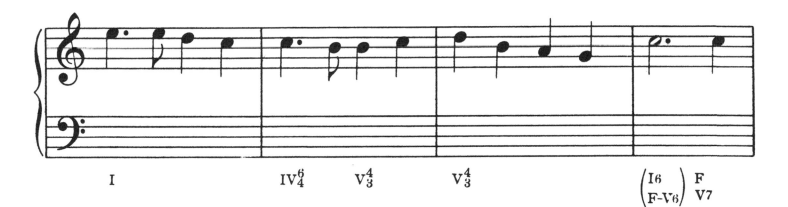

$$I \qquad \binom{V_4^6}{G\text{-}I_4^6} \qquad G\text{-}I_4^6 \qquad G\text{-}V7 \qquad \binom{V_4^6}{G\text{-}I_4^6} \quad V_3^4$$

$$I \qquad IV_4^6 \quad V_3^4 \qquad V_3^4 \qquad \binom{I6}{F\text{-}V6} \; \begin{matrix} F \\ V7 \end{matrix}$$

$$\binom{IV_4^6}{F\text{-}I_4^6} \qquad I \qquad IV_4^6 \quad V_3^4 \qquad I$$

Work Sheet

1 What is the basis of our harmonic system?

_____

2 What is meant by CHORD PROGRESSION?

_____

_____

3 What makes a cadence PERFECT?

_____

4 What is the chord progression of an AUTHENTIC CADENCE?

_____   _____

5 What is the chord progression of a PLAGAL CADENCE?

_____   _____

6 What is a cadence called which has more than two chords?

_____

7 On the staff below, mark the AUTHENTIC cadences with numerals and inversions.

8 On the staff below, write the cadences marked.

IV_4^6 I   IV6 I_4^6 IV   I6   IV V_4^6 I6

Lesson Five

FRÉDÉRIC CHOPIN

(1810-1849)

Chopin was born in Poland on February 22, 1810. Both of his parents were musical and saw that he was given good instruction in music. When he was only eight years old, he played very difficult pieces with ease. He also composed pieces at that age.

When he was nineteen, he had completed a thorough education in music. He gave concerts in Vienna and other cities of Europe. When he played in Paris, he liked that city so well that he decided to live there.

He taught piano and gave yearly concerts. Many other fine musicians were his friends, Mendelssohn, Schumann, Liszt and others. His piano pupils loved to study with him because he was such a good teacher and brought out the beauty of music on the piano.

His compositions for the piano were successful at once. They were the first pieces written which were strictly PIANO MUSIC. Chopin was the first composer who did not use other effects in his music. For example, Beethoven used orchestral effects.

Chopin lived for a while on the island of Majorca where he composed a great deal of music. But he contracted tuberculosis there and returned to Paris.

Although he played as well as any other great artist, Chopin preferred to play for small audiences in salons rather than for large audiences in concert halls. However, when he returned from Majorca, he began to give many concerts. Because of his illness, the strain was too great, and he died at the age of thirty-nine.

All of Chopin's compositions were written for the piano. He really understood the piano, what it could do and how it could sound. This enabled him to write wonderful piano music. All of his music has beautiful melodies and harmonies and covers a great emotional range. Yet he gave very impersonal titles to these great masterpieces: Etudes, Preludes, Nocturnes, etc.

Chopin, Schumann and Liszt are considered the founders of modern piano technique.

Modulation and Related Keys

When you play a piece written in the Key of C and find some accidentals of F#, you are temporarily playing in the Key of G, but there is not enough of the composition in the Key of G to make changing the key signature worth while.

If a piece has the key signature of C but there are G# accidentals, the composition is either all in *a minor* or a part of it is. One way to find out is to look at the end of the composition. The cadence chord will tell you because it is probably the end of a PERFECT CADENCE and will have *do* in the soprano and bass.

A change of key but not key signature within a composition is called MODULATION.

The modulation is made from the signature key to a closely related key. By related we mean they have notes in common; they go together well. One key will have the keys of its dominant and subdominant notes and its relative minor and their relative minors as related keys. For example C major has G and F major and a, e and d minor as related keys.

The circle of fifths shows this plainly. Any three keys in order with their relative minors are related keys.

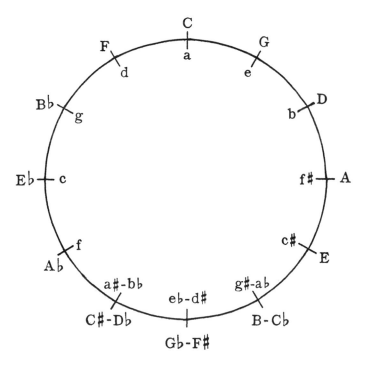

Name the Major and Minor related keys to the ones given.

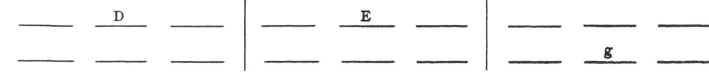

MODULATION is accomplished by the use of a **PIVOT CHORD**.

A **PIVOT CHORD** is a chord found in both keys.

In Book 2 we saw that C E G is the Tonic of the Key of C. It is the Subdominant of the Key of G, the Dominant of F.

On the staff below, write the numeral under each chord.

On the following staff, write a chord above each numeral.

Complete the following:

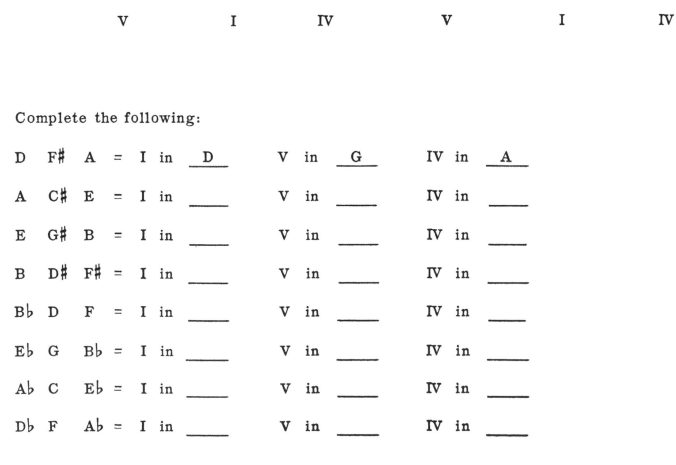

D   F# A = I in ___D___   V in ___G___   IV in ___A___

A   C# E = I in _____   V in _____   IV in _____

E   G# B = I in _____   V in _____   IV in _____

B   D# F# = I in _____   V in _____   IV in _____

Bb D F = I in _____   V in _____   IV in _____

Eb G Bb = I in _____   V in _____   IV in _____

Ab C Eb = I in _____   V in _____   IV in _____

Db F Ab = I in _____   V in _____   IV in _____

The following four measures of the *Choral* by Robert Schumann show the key signature of G. The second chord of the second measure is a PIVOT CHORD. It is G V and D I. This progresses through the D V7 to D I in measure three and again in measure four to form a Perfect Cadence and to establish the key of D which is the Dominant Key.

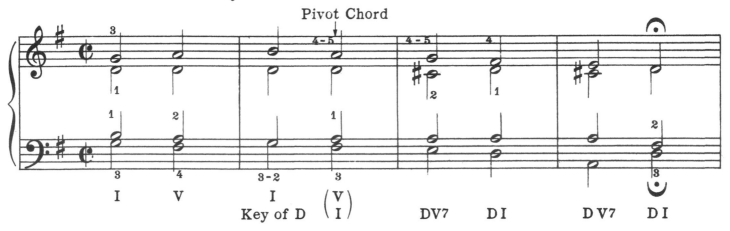

Notice that each tone has its own stem. This is called four-part VOICE writing. The top line of notes is the soprano. The other line of notes in the treble clef is the alto. The top notes of the bass clef are the tenor and the lower notes the bass. Play these measures. Can you transpose them to the Key of F?

The following are the first four measures of *The Happy Farmer* also by Robert Schumann. Only the fourth measure is in C which is the dominant key. Play this on the piano.

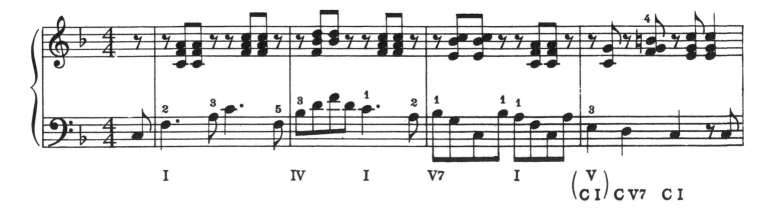

The following is part of *The Reaper's Song* by Robert Schumann. All of the chords are I, IV, V or V7 in C or G major.

Write the numeral under each chord. In measures 1-4 and 9-12, the upper two notes show which chord is used. The lower two notes are repeated for effect. Do not consider the small notes in between the chords for this exercise. Play this on the piano.

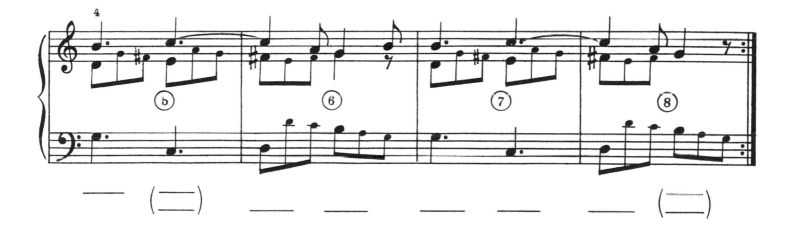

Notice the mixed cadence in measures 7 and 8.

Work Sheet

1 What three composers founded the modern piano technique?

_____

2 What is MODULATION? _____

_____

3 Complete the following:

Key signature	accidental	Modulated key
C	F♯	_____
G	C♯	_____
F	B♮	_____

4 Write in triads for the numerals below.

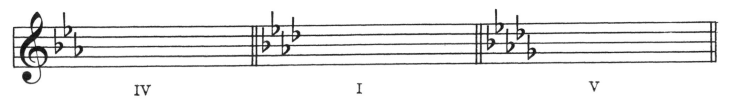

IV   I   V

5 Complete the key signatures and numerals for the following chord in three related keys.

6 Write the key signatures for the following chords.

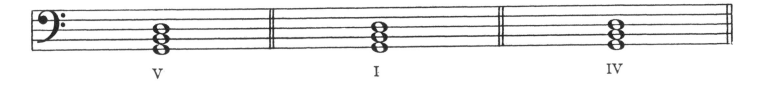

V   I   IV

Lesson Six

ROBERT SCHUMANN

(1810-1856)

Robert Schumann was born in Germany in 1810, the youngest son of a book seller who knew the boy was talented in music. Robert started studying the piano when he was seven years old and was composing when he was eleven years old.

When his father died, his mother decided he should study law and sent him to the University of Leipzig, but Robert did not want to be a lawyer and did not make good grades in law courses.

He really loved music and wanted to learn more about it. After two years in the university, his mother said he could work to become a musician. This made him very happy. He played for Frederich Wieck, a great teacher who recognized Robert's genius, and invited Schumann to live in his home.

Schumann was so anxious to become a concert artist that he practiced a great deal. He also invented a gadget to hold one finger while he exercised others. In working this way, one of his fingers was permanently injured. This meant he could not become a concert artist.

He then turned to composing. He married Clara Wieck, the daughter of Professor Wieck. Clara was a fine concert pianist. They had eight children.

In addition to composing, Schumann published a magazine about music and musicians. His ideas on how to practice and other information on music were widely read. He helped other musicians, especially Brahms. He taught at Leipzig with Mendelssohn, conducted orchestras, and occasionally went with his wife Clara on her concert tours. But he began to have headaches and eventually lost his mind. He spent the last two years of his life in a sanatorium.

Clara Schumann lived forty years after Robert died. She gave concerts of the music her husband had composed and helped to edit his music for publishers.

Schumann loved children and wrote many lovely pieces for them.

Keyboard Instruments

The **ORGAN** is the earliest known keyboard instrument. In 800 and 900 it had from eight to ten large keys which were pulled and pushed.

The **CLAVICHORD** which dates from around 1100 is the earliest known **STRINGED** keyboard instrument. The case was a wooden box two to five feet wide which could be set on a table or have legs. The strings ran the same direction as the keyboard. The tone was produced by a brass wedge (called a tangent) striking the strings. By the time of Bach, it was used mainly in Germany.

The **HARPSICHORD** usually had two keyboards or manuals. It was shaped like our grand piano. The strings were plucked by a quill to make the tones sound. Harpsichords date from around 1400 and were very popular until the early 1800s. In fact, even after the piano was in use, music published stated that it was for the Harpsichord or the Piano.

Harpsichords are being used again. Their fine tone blends well with stringed instruments for chamber music. Since much of our music was written for the instrument, musicians feel that the music should be played on it whenever possible.

Cristofori invented the piano, but it has gone through many changes before becoming the instrument it is today. Early pianos had several pedals on them for tone changes.

John Hawkins invented the **UPRIGHT** piano. He was an Englishman who moved to America and became an American citizen. His piano was shown in 1802 at Philadelphia. Mr. Hawkins also invented the mechanical pencil.

Upright pianos also went through many changes. At first they were about six feet tall. One was even called a giraffe piano! Another was called a piano sloping backwards because it did slope backwards. The pianist could then see the audience, and he could also turn pages by pressing his knee against a lever on this instrument.

At first pianos were built to order. Even today there are pianos built to order. They are very special and very expensive. Steinway built a piano for the White House. Baldwin built a golden piano for Moriz Rosenthal when he had been a concert artist for fifty years.

Compound Meter

In Book 2 we learned that METER is the way note values and accents are grouped in a measure.

SIMPLE METER compositions have 2, 3 or 4 as the top number of the time signature. A regular note is the beat unit.

COMPOUND METER has the upper figure of Simple Meter multiplied by three. The beat unit is a dotted note.

	Simple				Compound							
Duple	$\frac{2}{2}$	$\frac{2}{4}$	$\frac{2}{8}$	becomes	$\frac{6}{2}$	$\frac{6}{4}$	$\frac{6}{8}$	count	1	2		
Triple	$\frac{3}{4}$	$\frac{3}{8}$		becomes	$\frac{9}{4}$	$\frac{9}{8}$		count	1	2	3	
Quadruple	$\frac{4}{4}$	$\frac{4}{8}$	$\frac{4}{16}$	becomes	$\frac{12}{4}$	$\frac{12}{8}$	$\frac{12}{16}$	count	1	2	3	4

There are two main reasons for having compound meter:
  1 Division of Accents   2 Ease of notation

Examples of counting and accents and beat units follow.

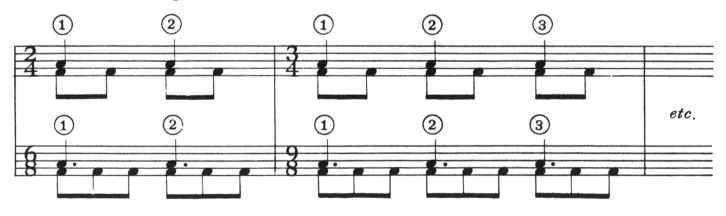

To divide the beat unit – In Simple meter, divide by 2.

In Compound meter, divide by 3.

Counting

Counting is most important. Although the time signature gives the beat unit, which means one count for each beat, we often count more than one for a beat. How we count depends on how notes are arranged in each beat.

Half or *and* may be used: *one half two half,* or *one and two and.* Sometimes both are used: one and half and. But usually if a beat is divided into four for counting, 1, 2, 3, 4 is used.

In some cases we count within the beat while learning in order to hold the notes accurately. If the tempo is rapid, we change the count to one per beat later.

Always count while playing. When we play for others, this habit of counting to ourselves (silently) will keep our minds and ears on our playing and will help us always to play well.

We must also remember the meter. Many compositions do not have the counting begin on beat one. It is important to count according to the meter.

The two examples below show the counting and the meter. They are *The Poor Orphan* and *The Hunting Song,* both by Robert Schumann. Play and *count this music.*

Below are four measures of *Sweet and Low*. **A** is compound meter. **B** shows how difficult this song would be if it were written in simple meter.

A (Count 1 2 3 4 5 6)

B (Count ?)

$\frac{6}{8}$ time is often used to express motion. Songs of the sea are usually in this meter. The
faster dance rhythm of the early Gigues are often in compound meter.

The following are measures from a Gigue by Telemann. Play this on the piano. Mark the
numerals of the chords under the beat notes of the bass. Watch for the key modulation.

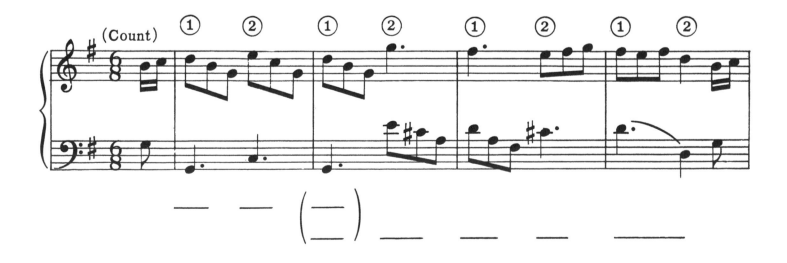

The METRONOME was invented in 1815 by John Maelzel or Mälzel.

This machine measures the time or duration of notes by means of a pendulum which swings back and forth a number of times per minute according to where the weight is placed on the pendulum opposite a graduated scale. Today many metronomes are electric.

Beethoven was the first composer to use the metronome. However, he said the figures which indicate tempo at the beginning of his compositions are merely a general idea. Very few compositions are played in strict time all the way through.

This deviation of time throughout a composition is important. The control of tempo shows musicianship. There are many occasions in most pieces to alter the rhythm by slight pauses at the ends of phrases, by ritardandos or accelerandos, by relative lengths of time for fermatas, and by rubatos.

ACCENT is the stress of one tone over another. This stress is usually made by playing a note louder or longer.

1 DYNAMIC accent is stress by means of WEIGHT. One tone is played louder than others.

    a) Regular dynamic accents fall on beat one and other beats which are normal to stress according to the number of beats in a measure.

    b) Irregular dynamic accents fall on weak beats.
        Syncopation is an irregular accenting of beats.

Syncopation upsets the normal pulse:

    1. By holding the strong beat from a weak beat.

    2. By having rests on strong beats.

    3. By stressing weak beats.

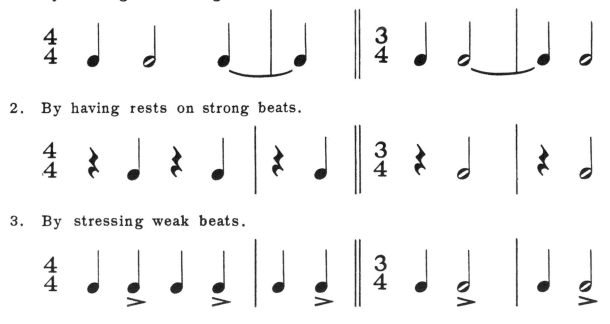

2 AGOGIC accent is stress by means of TIME. A tone is held longer than the notation for it. The word rubato or a fermata indicate this accent.

We have tapped out the rhythms of various melodies and have seen how important rhythm is in the melody. We have been able to tell the name of the piece just by hearing the rhythm tapped.

Because each note of a melody tells us how long to hold a note as well as its pitch, MELODY is the MOVEMENT of tones plus rhythm.

Here is part of the melody of *The Happy Farmer* showing the two parts of MELODY separately.

The MOVEMENT is chord-wise or scale-wise.

Every note of the melody shown above *The Happy Farmer* is all part of the chords.

But some melodies move scale-wise and have notes which are not part of the chords but which move between notes of the chords.

A part of *Träumerei* by Robert Schumann is given below. The scale notes which are not part of the chords are circled.

Write the chord numerals on the lines below the bass staff.

Work Sheet

1 What is the earliest stringed keyboard instrument known?

_____

2 What kind of note is the beat unit for Compound Meter?

_____

3 What is done to the top figure in Simple Meter to make it Compound Meter?

_____

4 Which accent is caused by stressing normal beats?

_____

5 Which accent is caused by changing the time value?

_____

6 What is the result of accenting other than normal beats?

_____

7 Of what two things is melody made?

_____

8 By what number can you divide the beat unit of

   a)   Simple meter _____

   b)   Compound meter _____

9 What are the two main reasons for Compound Meter?

   a)   _____

   b)   _____

Lesson Seven

FRANZ LISZT

(1811 - 1886)

Franz Liszt was born in Hungary. His father taught him to play the piano. At nine years of age, Franz gave his first public concert. After his second concert, wealthy people gave money for his musical education in Vienna.

Liszt took piano lessons from Carl Czerny. He also played for Beethoven who was delighted with his playing.

When he was twelve years old, he gave his first concert in Vienna. He was so wonderful that his father took him to Paris to the Conservatory. The head of this famous conservatory knew that Franz had passed every entrance examination, but he would not let Liszt study there because he did not like child prodigies.

From that time on, Liszt took no more lessons but kept practicing and developing his genius by himself. He did study harmony and composition. He was in the high est musical society in Paris.

When Liszt was a child, he realized he was a genius, and it made him humble. He felt he should serve both music and musicians. This he did, all of his life.

As a teacher, he taught hundreds of pianists. Even when he became very famous, he still taught but did not charge for the lessons. More than half of the pianists who were famous between 1875 and 1925 were his pupils. He made the word RECITAL popular.

He was the greatest of all pianists. His style of piano playing was beyond anything anyone else could do. He had an amazing technique, but he also played the music of a composer to bring out the most beautiful ideas of the composer. Audiences adored Liszt. Sometimes he had two pianos on a stage and he would play one and then the other. In this way every person in the audience was able to see his hands.

As a composer, he created the Symphonic Poem. He also introduced a new style of harmony and melody that he called "music of the future." Some of his music was dramatic and loud; some of it is dreamy and beautiful. Most of his music is quite difficult to play.

Intervals

Review: an INTERVAL is the distance from one note to another.

an INTERVAL is the difference in pitch between two tones.

an interval is MEASURED by counting the lines and spaces from one note to the other including both notes.

MAJOR INTERVALS are 2 3 6 7.

PERFECT INTERVALS are 1 4 5 8.

MINOR INTERVALS are one half-step smaller than Major intervals.

DIMINISHED INTERVALS are one half-step smaller than Perfect or Minor intervals. Mark these.

AUGMENTED INTERVALS are one half-step larger than Perfect or Major intervals. Mark these.

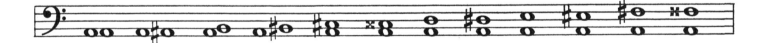

On the staff below

a) write the size and type of intervals given.

b) add an upper note to form the intervals.

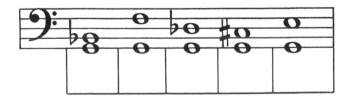

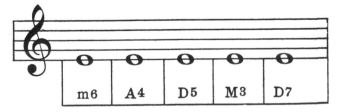

| m6 | A4 | D5 | M3 | D7 |

Write the type and size of the intervals given below.

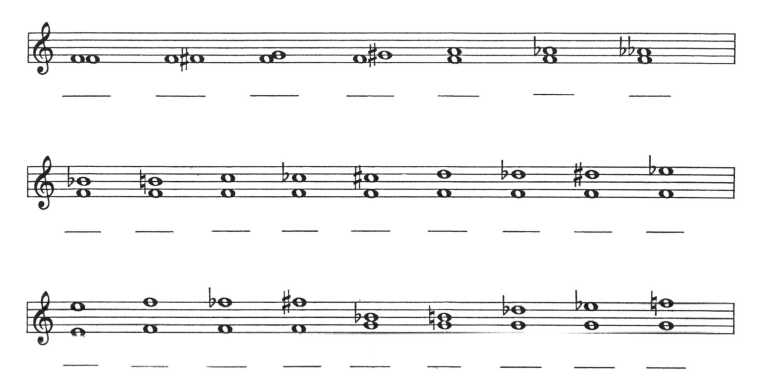

On the staff below, write an upper note to form the intervals marked.

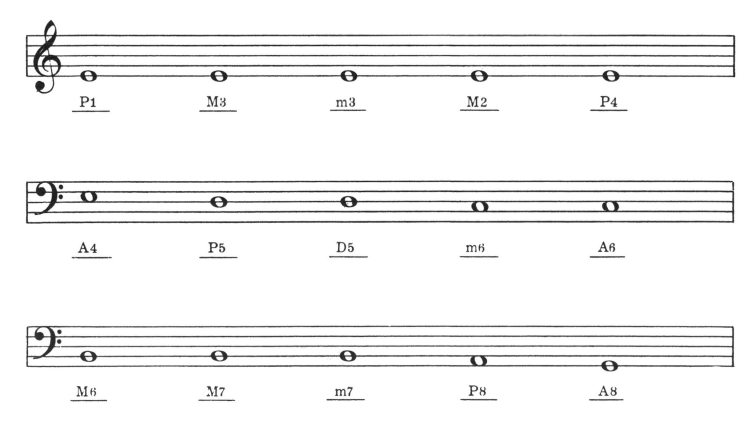

Inverted Intervals

INVERTING means reversing the notes of the intervals.

There are two ways to invert an interval:

   1 Write the lower note an octave higher.

   2 Write the upper note an octave lower.

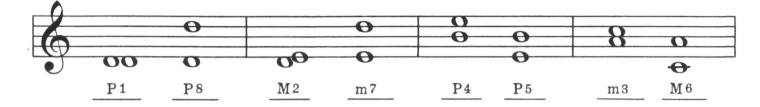

An interval and its inversion add to 9.

     1 becomes 8 = 9; 2 becomes 7 = 9; 3 becomes 6 = 9; 4 becomes 5 = 9, etc.

Major intervals invert to minor intervals.

Minor intervals invert to major intervals.

BUT Perfect intervals invert to perfect intervals. They remain perfect.

Write the size and type of the following intervals.

A diminished interval inverts to an augmented interval.

An augmented interval inverts to a diminished interval.

On the staff below mark the size and type of the intervals and their inversions.

Beethoven used many inverted intervals in his compositions.

Watching for these composing devices helps us learn pieces more easily.

Work Sheet

The following is a chart of the most used intervals:

1 ———————— Perfect or Augmented

4   5   8 ———— Perfect, Diminished, Augmented

2   6 ———————— Major, Minor, Augmented

3   7 ——————— Major, Minor, Diminished

1   On the staffs below, write the used intervals on D.

P1   A1   P4   D4   A4   P5   D5   A5

P8   D8   A8   M2   m2   A2   M6   m6   A6

M3   m3   D3   M7   m7   D7

2   To what does a Major interval invert? _____

3   To what does a Diminished interval invert? _____

4   To what does a Perfect interval invert? _____

5   To what total do inverted intervals add? _____

6   Which great composer often used intervals and their inversions in his compositions?

_____

Lesson Eight

JOHANNES BRAHMS

(1833-1897)

Brahms was born in Hamburg, Germany. He was first taught by his father who was a musician. Brahms gave his first public concert when he was fourteen years old. He included a composition of his own at that concert.

He had to earn his own living at this early age. It was difficult for him to get work as a classical player so he earned his living by playing in taverns. However, a great violinist heard him and hired him as his accompanist. They traveled throughout Germany where others heard Brahms and admired his great playing.

He met Liszt and many other musicians. Schumann became his very good friend and wrote about him to help him become better known. Brahms became very successful, and his music was played everywhere. Concert halls were crowded whenever he played.

Brahms did not compose music in the style of the future as Liszt did. He knew a great deal about the style, but he preferred to use the classic forms for his music. Many people felt that nothing new could be added after Beethoven in these classic forms, but Brahms proved he could expand them in his own great way.

Brahms also would take themes of other composers and write variations on them. His 51 exercises are played by advanced students of piano. He also edited music for music publishers.

His Lullaby or Cradle Song, which is a very lovely composition, was written for a friend to sing to her new baby. He also wrote many Hungarian Dances. His music has varied rhythms.

When he was forty-five years old, he grew a beard because he did not want to shave nor to wear collars. He was a self-educated man in literature and other subjects. He was a very brilliant person.

During his lifetime, people began talking about the three Bs for Bach, Beethoven and Brahms. He did not like this because he was humble about his genius and underrated himself. He honored Bach and Beethoven and felt that they were far above him. Today we recognize the intricate beauty of his music.

Here is the *Old French Song* by Tchaikovsky

What is the Key?_____ Write the Time **Signature**.

Write numerals under each chord.

What type of cadence is in measures 7-8?_____

and in measures 23-24?_____

Count this music as you play.

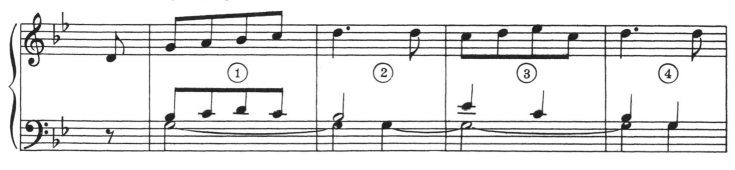

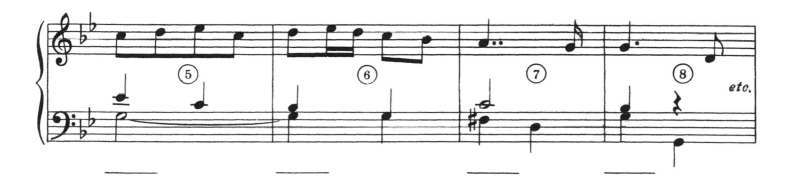

This piece is *The Lonesome Road*. Write in the time signature and the chords.   Notice the
SONG FORM is A   A   B   A. Play what you have written. Then transpose it to
other keys.

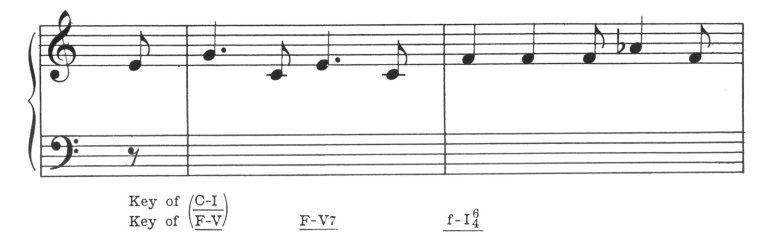

Key of $\left(\dfrac{\text{C-I}}{\text{F-V}}\right)$ F-V7   f-I$\frac{6}{4}$

Fine

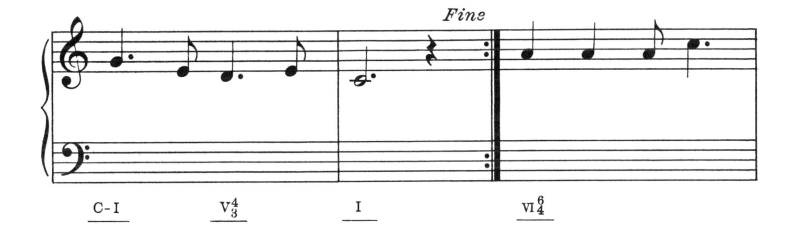

C-I   V$\frac{4}{3}$ I   VI$\frac{6}{4}$

D.C. al Fine

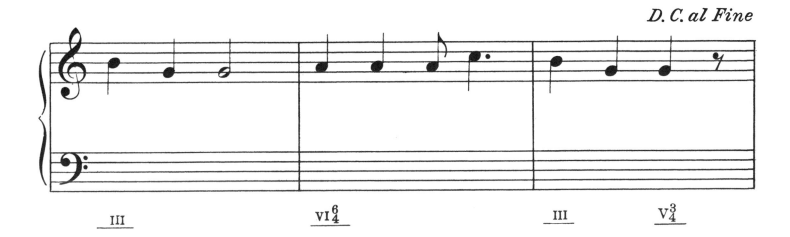

III   VI$\frac{6}{4}$ III   V$\frac{3}{4}$

Complete the writing of the following piece. Put in the Key and Time signatures. Play it and transpose it.

Examination

1 What is the same for RELATIVE MAJORS and MINORS? _____

_____

2 What is the same for PARALLEL MAJORS and MINORS? _____

_____

3 Write the Key-tones for Majors and Relative Minors on the following circle of fifths.

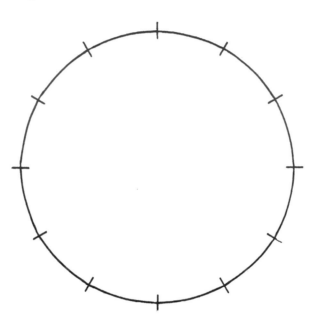

4 On the following staff, write the Key Signatures for the Parallel Majors and Minors.

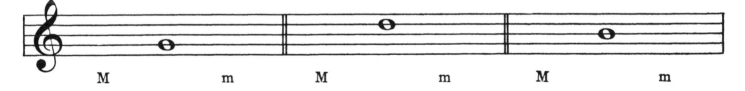

M   m   M   m   M   m

5 On the following staff, write the Harmonic Minor scale of G one octave up and down.
   Use the bass clef.

6 Why is this form difficult to sing? _____

_____

7 On the staff below, write the Melodic E Minor Scale one octave up and down. Use the treble clef.

8 Write M for Major or m for minor under each triad below.

9 Which interval is changed to make a Major Triad become a Minor Triad? _____

_____

10 Which intervals never become minor intervals? _____

_____

11 Which intervals do become minor? _____

How is this done? _____

12 What was Schubert called? _____

_____

13 Which composer wrote only piano music? _____

_____

14 Who was the greatest concert artist? _____

_____

15 Who married the daughter of his teacher? _____

_____

16 Write the Scale of Triads in the Key of F Major. Use the treble clef.
Write the numeral under each triad. Show the diminished triad.

17 In Major Scales, which scale degrees have Major Triads? _____

18 In Major Scales, which scale degrees have Minor Triads? _____

19 In Major Scales, which is the diminished triad? _____

What interval makes it diminished? _____

20 Why is it important to know about triads? _____

_____

_____

21 What is a PERFECT CADENCE? _____

_____

22 Which chords form an AUTHENTIC CADENCE? _____

23 Which chords form a PLAGAL CADENCE? _____

24 What is a chord progression? _____

_____

25 Name the parts of four-part harmony?

_____   _____

_____   _____

26 Which three great composers are considered to be the founders on modern piano technique?

_____

51

27 Write in the related keys on the lines below.

a) _____ __A__ _____ _____   b) _____ _____ _____

   _____ _____ _____   _____ __f__ _____

c) __G__ _____ _____   d) _____ _____ _____

   _____ _____ _____   _____ _____ __e__

28 What is MODULATION? _____

_____

_____

29 What is a PIVOT CHORD? _____

_____

30 Write triads in the three keys above the following numerals.

        IV   I   V

31 If a composition is in the key of B♭ and you find accidentals of E♮, what is the

   modulated key? _____

32 What is done to a note when it is the beat unit for Compound meter? _____

_____

33 What is done to the TOP figure of a time signature to make it Compound? _____

_____

34 By what number can you divide a beat unit

   a) In Simple meter? _____

   b) In Compound meter? _____

35 Of what TWO things is Melody made? _____

_____

36 What is an INTERVAL? _____

_____

37 What TWO kinds of intervals are found in a Major Scale? _____

_____

38 How is a MINOR interval formed? _____

_____

39 How is a DIMINISHED interval formed? _____

_____

40 How is an AUGMENTED interval formed? _____

_____

41 What is an INVERTED interval? _____

_____

42 On the staff below, write the inverted interval for each interval given. Then write the size and type of both in each section.

43 Write the size and type under each interval on the following staff.

44 What does an inverted Major third become? _____

Ländler

45

Cornelius Gurlitt, Op. 130

a) Write in the time signature.

b) Name the roots of the chords for each measure.

(1) _____ (2) _____ (3) _____ (4) _____ (5) _____ (6) _____ (7) _____ (8) _____

c) Mark numerals under the chords.

d) Which two measures have minor chords? _____

e) How is the chord in measure 6 used? _____

f) Name the type of cadence in measure 7 – 8 _____

g) Check if it is Perfect _____ or Imperfect _____